THE ROUNDING

*For Sally
with thanks for all you did
to our world at Seabury —
Blessings, Renée*

ALSO BY RENNIE McQUILKIN

An Astonishment and an Hissing
North Northeast
We All Fall Down
Counting to Christmas
Learning the Angels
Passage
Getting Religion
Private Collection
First & Last
The Weathering: New & Selected Poems
Visitations
Going On
A Quorum of Saints
Dogs
North of Eden: New & Collected Poems
Afterword
The Readiness
Seabury Seasons
Coming Through

THE ROUNDING

A BOOK OF DAYS

Poems by

Rennie McQuilkin

Antrim House
Bloomfield, Connecticut

Copyright © 2022 by Robert Rennie McQuilkin

Except for short selections reprinted for purposes of
book review, all reproduction rights are reserved.
Requests for permission to replicate should
be addressed to the publisher.

Library of Congress Control Number: 2022930056

ISBN: 978-1-943826-95-7

First Edition, 2022

Printed & bound in the USA

Book design by Rennie McQuilkin

Front cover photograph by Ian Clark:
"Blood Moon Behind the Steeple"

Author photograph by Hunter Neal, Jr.

Antrim House
860.519.1804
AntrimHouseBooks@gmail.com
www.AntrimHouseBooks.com
400 Seabury Dr., #5196, Bloomfield, CT 06002

THANKS AND A PREFACE

This book is dedicated to the splendid staff at Seabury.

My thanks to the editors of the following publications in which these poems first appeared in earlier versions:

Connecticut River Review: "On the Enlarging of Diminishment"
Here: "Ultima Thule" (forthcoming)
Voices: "For Joan," "Roots"

I am grateful to early readers of the poems in this book, in particular Sarah, my dear wife, and Katharine Carle. They have offered very helpful suggestions. I would also like to thank Ian Clark for his splendid photograph appearing on the book's front cover.

In this Book of Days, once again presenting poems in chronological order, I pick up where I left off toward the end of July, 2020 in my previous book, *Coming Through*.

Rennie McQuilkin
Bloomfield, CT
February, 2022

Table of Contents

Prologue: *The Longing* / 3

What I'd Like / 5
Making a Fist / 6
Amphibian Affair / 7
Against the Storm / 8
The Flower Woman / 9
Pancake Morning / 10
Murder in the Glen / 11
For Ruth Bader Ginsberg / 12
All Creatures / 13
From the Eye of a Drone over a Norwegian Fjord / 14
Code / 15
The Roosting / 16
Suspension / 17
Second Growth / 18
For the Giant Pacific Octopus / 19
Happy Returns / 20
For the Last Cricket / 21
The Opening / 22
Family / 23
Team / 24
Winter Garden, Boxing Day / 25
Dem Bones, A New Year's Song / 26
New Year's Morning 2021 / 27
Resolution / 28
Birthings / 29
Something / 30
Cross Country / 31
On the Enlarging of Diminishment / 32
Ultima Thule / 33
There All Along / 34
Mountain Rides / 35
Mardi Gras / 36

Waiting / 37
Immanentizing the Eschaton / 38
The Price of Heaven / 40
Sunny Side / 41
Breakfast Ritual / 42
White Throat / 43
The Recycling / 44
The Terror / 45
Easter Offering / 46
Hyla Crucifer / 47
Another Good Friday / 48
Except / 49
For Joan / 50
Flood / 51
Her Family / 52
My Yellow Brick Road / 53
The Brooding / 54
Whose Porch This Is / 55
Firefly / 56
Paradise Lost at the Retirement Center / 57
An Anniversary Remembered / 58
The Art of Walking / 60
Loss / 61
Logging In / 62
Replacement / 63
Thelma / 64
Roots / 65
Grades / 66
Inflation / 67
The Clock and I / 68
The Lady and the Moose / 69
The Lifting / 70
The Birthing / 71
A Meditation on Time / 72
Blood Moon over the Cathedral / 73
A Prayer for Advent / 74
Solstice Celebration in a Time of Pandemic / 75

Another Birth / 76
Praise Song for Skunk Cabbage / 77
Joy / 78
Connection / 79
The Waiting / 80

About the Author / 83
About the Book / 84

When true simplicity is gain'd,
To bow and to bend we will not be asham'd,
To turn, turn will be our delight,
Till by turning, turning we come round right.

Shaker Elder Joseph Brackett

THE ROUNDING

PRELUDE

The Longing

I scrawl and scrawl, looking for words
buried deep as a Painted wintering
under mud. May it rise in season,
stretch its long neck, take in the sun
and utter truth in a still voice so small
I must pay bestial attention.

What I'd Like

I'd like to write a poem
as clear as a mountain stream
you could drink from and see
cleanly to the sandy bottom –

glints of mica, speckled stones,
gold bones of aspen leaves,
fish bowls with chinook eggs
glittering like their maker,

all this stippled stuff mingling
with clouds, the sky, the over-
hanging poplar leaves reflecting
silver as they swivel in the wind

whose ripples crease the scene
then subside, revealing again
the depths and heights I'd like
my poem to fathom.

7.23.20

Making a Fist

I've read about a worried child told she wasn't dying
since she could still make a fist. That was good news
to the child, but I was worried this morning
when my hand wouldn't close, except for one finger
that couldn't uncurl. I lay there trying to straighten
it out, and when I did, with a painful snap,
I worked my hands, trying to bunch them into fists,
drifted back to sleep, and from my corner
said to the Adversary, bare-knuckled, "Come on . . ."

7.24.20

Amphibian Affair

Widows both, they are out late, bent low,
hands on knees like short front legs
at the edge of a cricket-singing koi pond,

hearing a different song,
looking for the source, and yes, there –
a gold throat ballooning and ballooning

and gilt stripes swept back from the eyes
of a lithe green singer
able to make any commoner a princess.

7.28.20

Against the Storm

for Lorrie and Chuck

The pestilence of 2020 directs them,
he to a new life of painting focused
on lighthouses.

He sets them in windows facing the sun.
When its rays level with their translucent life-
saving lanterns, they shine for anyone at sea.

And she has created globes of colorful yarn
recalling the rope sailors coil around heavy stones:
"Monkey Fists"

attached to hawsers they throw to those on wharfs
who pull them in for safe harboring
no matter what storms might batter them.

She has set out bowls of her own Monkey Fists
like many-colored hydrangeas
assembled to preserve lost beauty, haul us back to it.

8.28.20

The Flower Woman

for BJ

The woman who ministers to flowers and bushes
around the rim of the pond she superintends
colors the world in accord with the turning of
the planet. She lives in league with the seasons,
plants and weeds, prunes and trains her climbers

timely, for the love of it and for neighbors
who circle her arena in three-tiered apartments –
and for others depending on her: wasps and bees,
ruby-throateds, swallowtails, monarchs, goldfinch.

She is up early, fertilizing, watering, talking softly
to the fish she feeds, the frog she accompanies.
This is not easy. She holds the small of her back
after setting forth earlier to superintend the dawn,
the sun-riven mist above East Meadow.

Afternoons, she branches out to highways in need
of her attention – so much obscuring violets, vetch,
primroses, buttercups:
beer cans, whiskey flasks, candy wrappers, detritus
of amorous exploits from the night before . . .
She shoulders her take in clattering burlap bags.

If only I did more than write about it. Can't blame her
for wanting less palaver.

9.10.20

Pancake Morning

I wake to the whack of my grandmother's axe out back,
quartering halved splits of hickory to heat the range.
It's Sunday, Pancake Day, and she'll need a hot griddle.

The first rays of sun glitter on the falling axe a second
before its sharp report and the thunk of stove-size chunks
piling up around her feet to stoke the old Ironheart.

Warming by the stove, I see a violet shadow
of woodsmoke swirl up the trunk of the silver maple
outside the kitchen, cast by the low and golden sun.

Grandmother holds an iron griddle above the stovetop,
circling it side to side in an eccentric orbit
to spread the umber bacon fat as dawn coats the sky.

Now the greased skillet spits and sizzles – time for the first
cream-colored batter. When it's freckled with small bubbles,
she flips it, revealing a round of amber gold in league

with the morning sun. About its edges is a lighter ring
like the glow around the sun looking in through the east window.
A glaze of light amber syrup repeats the sheen of the glass.

9.13.20

Murder in the Glen

On one of the peaceful trails we residents frequent,
a murder has occurred. In the rash of reports
unleashed, the unhappy event dominates
conversation in this time of plague.

The question is whether it was a rat, a weasel or a mink
that seized the young rabbit by the throat,
dragged it into the underbrush. Emerging consensus
would have it a mink. Why does this seem pleasing?

Maybe we elders remember the mink
stoles our grandmothers wore to church, their velvety
softness we touched when our grannies returned
from drinking the blood and eating the flesh.

That was called communion, and the mink a lovely
part of it. We know better than to wear animal pelts
around our necks now, but the memory lingers.
Let it be a mink that did it, fed its young.

May we too go in no less style.
May it not be the plague that takes us by the throat
when our time is up, but something whose bestiality
allows us to find a kind of fearful beauty in it.

9.18.20

For Ruth Bader Ginsberg (1933-2020)

When we heard the news, we couldn't bear to be
by ourselves. Some of us gathered by the hundreds
before the Supreme Court of the land where you fought
so long for our rights, *Equal Justice* writ large overhead.
We broke spontaneously into *Amazing Grace,*
knowing you were more than we deserved and now

had lost – you brave, whimsical, richly reserved justice
with a voice like a shofar in a tiny body calling us to rise
to a humanity we so often denied. Oh *Notorious RBG,*
how apt that you left us on Rosh Hashanah,
that day ensuring special grace for all who die on it.

Despite the bone-pickers converging to rip apart
your legacy, your brilliant opinions and dissents
ringing out above the political din
will sing sweetly in the echoing chambers of history.

9.19.20

All Creatures

Here they assemble, great and small:
a black bear whose three sleek cubs
regard the place as a playground,
climbing the pine like a jungle gym;

beak-jabbing, bullet-fast hummingbirds,
turkeys and all manner of groundlings
entirely aware of each other, but not
begrudging. Peaceable, this kingdom.

I could be Adam naming the animals
passing between rhodos and japonica
or Noah admitting them into the ark
of my heart.

9.21.20 (original 6.1.17)

From the Eye of a Drone over a Norwegian Fjord

Better than merely human eyes, the drone sees
churning cascades, jagged boulders and cliffs
tolerating insect-size climbers
clinging to stone, bravely waving as if to say
hei og hade, hello and goodbye.

Such small life will not be here for long, but Earth
will last as long as the sun permits, spinning bravely
on the edge of a minor galaxy in one of an untold
number of universes, themselves hanging on until
the next retreat to Nothing, ready to explode again.

9.22.20

Code

for Martha

I seldom saw her those days we walked
different routes. But on occasions I visited
the grave of a friend we shared, and there
I'd find her in pebbles and pinecones she'd
left on the headstone, by which I set mine,
knowing she'd answer with her own. Now
that the distance between us has grown,
I set out these words like bits of code
and hope she'll answer in scuds of cloud.

9.23.20

The Roosting

for Robin

My son the bibliophile speaks pure
Wyandotte and Plymouth Rock,
sitting amid his bevy of hens,
allowing them free range on him.
They take turns roosting on his head
as if it's a giant egg they need to brood,
even their claws warm on his skull.
They see themselves in his eyes,
discuss the dirt of the day with him.

9.25.20

Suspension

Strange how it always seems to happen.
A heron stands in for my departed father,
looking my way insistently, not minding
its own business that first day without him;

a loon floats back and forth below the bluff
behind my friend's house on Grand Isle, not
diving or working the waters, just being there
for days after her husband's death.

No doubt we read too much into these things,
but this morning, a few minutes before
the service for my friend, a late Monarch drifts
(doesn't dart or flit but *drifts*) over a pond,

before a few last takings-in preceding its long
migration to Mexico, riding thermals,
bound for Michoacan, one of a thousand thousand

Spirits of the Departed, they say, arriving
on the Day of the Dead.
Something in us deeper than reason,
simple as prayer, willingly suspends its disbelief.

9.26.20 (for Margy and Martha)

Second Growth

for Bill and Penny

He and she have recovered from Covid,
he amazingly back from the hospital
after so long away we feared for him
while she languished, bereft in isolation.
Now I see them walking hand in hand,
enjoying the last of the year, the asters,
the second blooming of rhododendron . . .

Every day he waters the flowers she loves,
Montauk Daisies and pink Lantana
dry from drought. She is a brightening,
her second blossoming as vivid as his.

10.6.20

For the Giant Pacific Octopus

Praise this octopus, inky creature that it is,
with its three hearts and eight arms,
each arm with a large brain knowing
many ingenious tricks.

Like all wild things, it kills only to survive.
In its off-hours the octopus loves
to play and will dance with the same fish
it ate that morning. It likes to dress up
in a suit of shells to say *Ha!* to sharks.

Divers who hang around a giant octopus
long enough to be seen as harmless
are fascinating to this inquisitive creature
and find that it can cuddle lovingly.

Which is, in a way, how a female octopus ends
her life, spending four years embracing her eggs,
eating nothing and slowly dying as she waves
her arms over the unborn, wafting life to them.

10.11.20

Happy Returns

They are dancing in the streets
and kissing complete strangers
like VJ Day. The cars are honking,
bells ringing from every church,
parades breaking out . . .

The long reign of Chaos is over:
the emperor has been shown to
have no clothes. He is ranting
but we are not listening –
we are imbibing bubbly

at the edge of the wild wood
bordering a meadow where a lone
celebrant is looping the loop,
barrel-rolling, spinning and diving
his model Spitfire.

Our hearts do their own stunts
while about us Fall flies its colors.
We drink it all in.

11.8.20

For the Last Cricket

I will feed you what you love most –
bits of carrot, orange, and apple.
Please come in, warm up,
rub one wing against the other
like a field hand sharpening a scythe.
I want that whetting to ring all winter.

11.13.20

The Opening

for Kathy

Windows have become my world –
I look out from mine at theirs
across the pond, six picture windows,
each with its own display. I like the one
with circus animals lining the sill
straight from the big top of their collector.
Through fancy's window I see them
perform all night: tigers dive
fiery hoops, bears dance, seals applaud . . .

Two smaller windows hedge the one
where the animals line up all day, waiting,
both windows with shades drawn at night.
At daybreak I see the shades,
first one, then the other, tremble slightly
and slowly rise like eyes opening to
take in the day, adjusting to its demands.
The circus animals freeze in place – but only
until the night sets them free.

11.19.20

Family

after a BBC special

High in the Atlas Mountains of Morocco
a blizzard descends on an exiled orangutan,
a Barbary Macaque sitting alone, a king once,
who now must die, shunned and isolated,
no teeth left to fight or crack the rinds of fruit,
starving and freezing in the zero of winter.
What happens next

is a sign of the way our forebears survived.
This deposed, broken-nosed macaque
must once have been so loved by the young
he cradled and fed, as is the way with his kind,
that a troop of them from God-knows-where
arrive, touch lips to his, embrace him and create
a life-saving huddle to fend off the freeze.

The orangutan and I might as well be brothers,
so humped and crippled am I, and always cold,
my toes curled, discolored and numb.
But I too am blessed.
Like his, my children have rushed in
and secured a safe perch for this old simian.
I feel their arms around me.

11.21.20

Team

for Jock

Two photos have stood for years
next to each other: in one
my brother pitches what seems
a beanball at me in the other photo,
where I read seriously, my book
spread open to the business day.

We lived in different worlds,
he six years younger and trouble,
I the do-gooder, straight man of
the family, something of a bore.
But DNA will out.

Today the photos seem to merge:
my book could be a catcher's mitt.
We are after all a team, a battery
working together. I call signals but
let him shake them off, try his sinker,
paint the corners. I bang my mitt.

11.30.20

Winter Garden, Boxing Day

for BJ

I am mulling wonders of the morning – the shifting
shadows and sheen on clapboard from a sun
just risen. I believe it is stirring roots and tubers.

Now it strikes this contraption my neighbor the gardener
has put out, odd C-shaped dangle of styrofoam globes
hung from a metal bishop's crook, defying explanation

until at dusk I see them light up green and red and blue
in a shifting pattern so mesmerizing I bless the Sun
they must have stored all day, these winter flowers.

12.26.20 (Boxing Day)

Dem Bones, a New Year's Song

I once stood for long minutes, delighted
by my x-rayed feet at Buddy Parks' shoe store.
And at sleep-overs, my friend and I shone flashlights
through the still thin skin of our 10-year-old hands,
happy that the truth of the world was so transparent.

Seventy-five years later I dread
the sight of an x-ray being pulled out of a drawer
like the tray in a morgue: my knee undressed, its pain
explained. Call me Dry Bones, now that I've seen
the spent joint, with which I'm told I should live.

I am reminded of my son's facetious, I trust, wish
to have my skeleton installed in his office, articulated
so that with the push of a button I'd dance a jig.
The thought of it tickles my funny bone,
but I guess I'll keep my bones a bit longer at home.

12.31.20

New Year's Morning 2021

At midnight last night, New Year's Eve 2020,
after an at-home lobster extravaganza,
I found myself in the Recycle Room
at this haven for the aged, removing remnants
of the feast, shell and toxic tomalley, wishing
to dispose of the year, whose horror persists.

This morning, having refilled the bird feeder
with a dessert of crushed, cream-colored peanuts,
I watch a winter goldfinch up from the field,
a bit gold-bibbed despite the desolation of winter,
gorging in this leanest of seasons. On and on
the finch indulges, eye to eye with me at the window.

I am listening to a simulcast of the New Year's Day
concert from Vienna, for encore "The Blue Danube,"
written by Strauss the Younger to revive the spirits
of the Viennese after the loss of so many
in a terrifying battle finishing off the previous year.
Like Strauss and like the finch, I will persevere.

1.1.21

Resolution

Whatever destruction our kind is intent on begetting,
the world beyond us is resolved to behave better.
Here is an orchid, long moribund, now at it again,

buds gorging on the winter sun,
vowing like novices to dress up in white wimples
with flush centers, the faces of satisfied nuns.

Now a visitation of winter goldfinch, this time
females olive as the orchid's buds, nodding their heads,
singing a slight *hello hello*.
Their olive shows tints of a gold they will unfold.

1.2.21

Birthings

for Kyra and great-granddaughter Ivy

It is the season to focus on what bears witness
to the Light: these round Myer Lemons weighing
down the bush that a year ago seemed a goner,
two of them saffron as tonight's full Moon,
and beside them an orchid, long without flowers,
whose apparently dead stem sent forth a shoot
bearing buds in fetal curl, heads enlarging
like the child's in Kyra's womb, newly come now
into the orchidaceous world.

1.9.21

Something

What joy is in the air? Mayhem's abroad
as ever, and the plague continues its ascent. Still...

What is it? The miraculous magi have gone home;
the Xmas tree behind a window across the pond
is down; ice covers the frozen fish;
only the barest purple hint of skunk cabbage is up.

The neighbor's white cat may know something.
She has resumed her position where the gifted tree
once stood. She is licking herself self all over,
taking in what grayed-out sun there is.

There's the sporadic tocking of drops from icicles,
and two minutes of daylight gained since yesterday.

But none of that entirely explains it, nor the angle
of the cold sun that has moved a degree to the north.
Now this *chick-a-dee-dee-dee*. I whistle back.
That is answer enough.

1.15.21

Cross Country

Blessed be the calm, the simplifying
blue glimmer of moonlight on fresh snowfall
cross-country skiing in Vermont.

I hear only the still small voice
of skis following the path of the skier before me.
Then the whirlwind explosion

of a grouse burrowed in snow. Crystals
drift down as the wing-battering fades, leaving
a silence more silent than before.

1.17.21

On the Enlarging of Diminishment

As parts of me fall away,
legs growing lean, chest caved,
might and mane diminishing,

I feel my spirit enlarge like
a child's birthday balloon let go
into the sky, its skin thinning,

the breath expanding within it
and all the colors expressing it
about to be released, scattered

into the greater world
full of a light more stunning
than its own.

1.24.21

Ultima Thule

NASA scientists reveled on New Year's Eve 2019 when a spacecraft launched in 2006 passed close enough to a tiny planet-in-progress, Ultima Thule, to send back images of this most distant object ever visited in the Solar System.

As the President of Earth's most benighted nation
celebrated another year of doing his best to desecrate
the planet, and as a man-made virus danced its way
toward the destruction of many millions
at midnight of a New Year's Eve ushering in
the direst year in recorded history,

a visionary robot had other ideas, training wide-open eyes
on the bowling-pin-shaped beginning of another planet
in the outermost regions of the Solar System,
merely 10 by 20 miles across but drawing in whatever
debris it could to rival its distant relative, Pluto.

That night the youngest member of the scientific team
reveling in victory envisioned a fast-motion progression
of Ultima Thule toward a state in which
microbes would try again, growing arms and legs
and living peaceably on the shores of an underground ocean,
guided by the ancient legend of another planet
whose beauty was undone by minds too big for their bodies.

1.25.21

There All Along

for E.A.M. (1908-2004)

We found them mid-February,
you and I – there all along
in the sumac by the river:

the bluebirds wintering over,
zags of them flashing indigo
among the rusty staghorns.

Some nights you too, Mother,
show yourself, never having left,
merely hiding out, bright as ever.

2.10.21

Mountain Rides

When I groan at the idea
of rising and shining
in my rusty state, working
toes skeptically,

lifting my knees
one by one, judiciously,
with a cracking of joints,
I think of then: children

rushing in at dawn, lifted
to the peak of my knees
for *Mountain Rides*
down slope. Off they go.

"Again, again!" Again
I rise and shine.

2.15.21

Mardi Gras

While Jupiter, bad boy of our System,
goes about pocketing cosmic stones
like the Brobdingnagian bully he is,
circled by puny cronies egging him on
to sling a stone at us and wipe us out,

I take my own playground pleasure in
these colorful little survivors of the last
extinction. Oh sing, gilt finches, sing
in the momentary Mardi Gras of today.
Forget Ash Wednesday.

2.18.21

Waiting

for Sah

What she wanted most was family.
Native-style, she crouched
and celebrated the crowning
of perfect children.

Time was unkind. One is in a home
for the brain-impaired, one in prison,
and one has turned against her.

The father of her children was unfit
and left, but she is forever their mother,
cares for them fiercely,
hopes time will take a turn in her favor.

Meanwhile, she pushes her boulder
uphill, does not blame its weight
or gravity, persists with all her might,

and waits.

2.19.21

Immanentizing the Eschaton

for Charlie

Why obscure it so cerebrally, Mr. Voegelin –
that code for "bringing Heaven down to earth,"
which I wish for this morning,
joyless as Job, watching a whirlwind whip
a blizzard over all things sheltering in place,

hiding the White Cat in Harriet's window
and the O in the ice of the pond feeding air
to fish. But lo, it stops, reveals both O
and Cat, half turned like Jehovah to Moses

as if to say how heavenly the moment,
How immanent this eschaton.

2.20.21

Backward

Watching this toy dog in the cafeteria
turning and turning before lying down
as today's Comfort Classic is dished out,

I am back with Derby, my 3-legged Dane
in 1947 as he circles himself
in the midst of my parents' living room,

clearing debris for a bed 2 million years ago,
taking me with him where he and I speak
the same tongue –

throat music we decipher happily,
a satisfied groaning.

2.20.21

The Price of Heaven

There's a spill of black sunflower seed
below the courtyard feeder
and pigeons are all over the fallen seed,
a steel-blue roiling like tide-turning sea.

I grind my teeth. There are no pigeons
in Heaven, which this arena clearly
is not. They ride one another indecently
and sit on rooftops – gargoyles excreting.

Why must they be fed? But look again.
The songbirds – juncos, sparrows, finches,
pretty little choristers – are also dining.
Seems you can't have Heaven without Hell.

2.24.21

Sunny Side

Nature's first green is gold – Robert Frost

How fine these sunny-sides this morning
collaborating with February's first gold.
Beyond the pond's sleeping red-gold koi,
BJ's old gilt-back ceramic tortoise
is out from under a lid of snow to ogle
the local gold. Crocus? Such amazement!
Last night's warm wind has whipped away
winter's decent snow-white covers,
exposing the pleasure of the young lovers.

2.25.21

Breakfast Ritual

I pick up Cording, his *Walking with Ruskin,*
coffee in one hand, book in the other,
and read to Sarah, a way of throwing off
the sleep I am still half involved in –
like uncoiling cordage
on the deck of a trawler, wrapping
the butt end of the line around a stone
to make a weighted "monkey fist"
and hurling it to a kindred spirit on the wharf
who hauls me in from the ocean on which
I floated all night. I am suddenly real enough
to get on with the day, read a little more,
and write to you, Dear Reader.

3.6.21

White Throat

for Kathy

Up goes the shade on her picture window,
a mind cleared of its debris by dreams.
Standing fast on the sill is a parade of
African animals,

and deeper within, the upright piano
with which the occupant hits the very notes
of a White Throat, making nothing of glass
dividing kith from kin.

Farther in, she is always young in vibrant
oils, pouting on the wall, restrained by her
mother, who paints her 80 years ago, keeping
her from breaking loose and climbing her tree,

where shortly she will hang out, watching
goings on of the wild, not her mother's now
where she has joined the greater world
of the White Throat and its ilk.

3.10.21

The Recycling

Blessèd scavengers, bacilli, wings from the sky
recycle inglorious remains, put death to use,
refine life's mess and welcome it to eternity.

Deep down where rot rounds into purity
detritus decaying prepares the way for bloom,
dirt restoring like scavengers, wings in the sky.

From deadest fell of timber, *nurse logs* lushly
feed saplings born of bacteria – skyward shoots
recycling the forest, welcoming it to eternity.

Circling above, buzzards and crows keep an eye
out for gore incensing high heaven and dive to
reuse it – wide-wingers scavenging, down from sky.

From possums changing dead mice to dime-size
young in birth pouches – to God giving us room
in the end – scavengers, bacilli, wings in the sky
refine life's mess and welcome it to eternity.

3.13.21

The Terror

At three a.m. she wakes him, crying out
in a voice so deep and stricken he barely knows it:
"We're losing them, losing them!" As if drowning,

she gasps for air, bruises him painfully, clutching
so hard he might be a lost spar floating mid-ocean.
Telling her she has had a bad dream enrages her.

When he switches position, she holds harder, cries
"Don't leave me, don't go!" He says no, he will stay,
try to help if she will say who it is they are losing.
"Don't you know? How could you not?"

At length she begins to breathe more slowly, deeply,
and falls asleep, her mild snoring like the lapping
of ocean waters quelled on a quiet shore . . .

In the morning she has no memory
of her night terror. They have coffee, chat amicably.
He reads aloud, as always. But he is undone.
All day he has been redoubling gifts of love for her.

3.19.21

Easter Offering

for Davida

The Peace Lily plant has thrust up white spathes
cupping stiff gold columns of pollen and birth parts
waiting for transport fruitlessly, given the lack of
winged creatures delighting in sweets of the lily.

Until today. A lepidopterist has filled the inner sky
over the plant with larger-than-life butterfly mobiles
vivid in every posture of adoration. I see them
descending to guzzle. Oh willing suspension.

3.21.21

Hyla Crucifer

Always before, I lived by marsh and meadow,
taking in the melt around a first skunk cabbage
pushing purply through the ice;
the old saw of the first jagged call of a redwing
fencing off his claim;
the crazed babble of fanatic, dime-size country
music-makers up from the muck . . .

who now am separated from the sweet stink and
riot of it all. Still, in this bell jar of the elderly
all thought is replaced by that memorized din –
the yearly resurrection of *Hyla crucifer,* each happily
bearing a cross on its back en route to perpetuity,
belying the silly name of *peeper* and boasting throatily
how it is alive against all the odds. It can't be quelled,
is busily making more of itself.

3.24.21

Another Good Friday

It's Friday. By chance, I check the time.
9:02 a.m.
They have hammered, have hoisted
the tree he is sharply crowned upon.

There's no comfort in the raucous song
of frogs bearing crosses on their backs.
I walk away from the bog,

visit another tree – not his – bursting
into blossom this early in spring,
a Star Magnolia, flowers white and gold-
centered in untimely triumph. I focus

on it to sweeten the taste of myrrh.
Whatever the future of the body brought
heavily down from the cross,
this burgeoning is sufficient resurrection

to give me heart. If only it might be a sign
of another.

4.2.21

Except

At Easter service today, the cynic in me
guesses it might have been a bear
that moved the boulder blocking the tomb,
too big for a man to budge – much as
a black bear twisted the steel bars defending
my son's chicken coop last night.

The cynic in me smiles ruefully – except . . .
except for that exquisite moment
in John's telling of the story – how one word,
"Mary," was all that was spoken, all
Mary Magdalene needed
to know the figure standing before her
was not the gardener she'd taken him for.
Her answer was equally simple: "Rabboni."

Such intimacy in those words, so much history
in their tone – to which we are not privy.

As for the rest, I cannot conquer disbelief – except . . .
despite me, the need to believe keeps my heart
slightly ajar. Please advise, Father John.

4.4.21

For Joan

(Joan Cox, 1925–2021)

The lights are out
in the rooms you appointed
so perfectly across the hall.

You've left a hole in my life
so dark it swallows light,
pulls me into it

and out the other side
into a world so bright
I see you again

on your porch overlooking
East Meadow,
immersed in it, dissolving

into its many shades of green,
losing yourself in beauty
before crossing the corridor,

fine as mist, inviting me to share.
Please come into the apartment
of my mind appointed

with your elegant furnishings,
everything you'll be wanting
to be at home in me forever.

4.14.21

Flood

for Laura

I was still terrified in 1946. The war
raged on in me. I'd seen too much
at Loew's before *Bambi* – war news,
disaster on disaster.

When rain fell heavily four days straight,
I feared what it meant. In one of my
dreams, torrents tore tiles from the roof
and I made sure my war surplus life raft
was ready, filled with dry surplus food.

Now, 75 years later, it goes on.
A friend of mine saw the waters rise
to the murals of San Marco in Venice
so high the flood touched the base
of a rainbow sending Good News to Noah.

My friend and I talk Apocalypse.
But she knows better than I what to do.
She does not blame the water.
It has its uses, she says, and collects it
in a rain barrel rigged to water her garden.

She has no illusions
but still goes on tending her garden.
She is nicking dozens of sweet pea seeds
with a nail clipper, splitting them just
enough to make the most of the waters.

4.16.21

Her Family

She startles him from sleep by appearing
in the wee hours dressed for travel,
announcing she has just seen a child home.

He holds her a long time, lost but knowing
she is becoming the essence of herself:
the mother, the protector.

Next morning she sleeps late, curled warmly.
At breakfast, they engage in a playful
naming of birds at the feeder:

Popeye for the gilt male goldfinch,
Olive for the protective, more secret female.
All things are becoming family.

4.23.21

My Yellow Brick Road

The war was over. Our answer to Uncle Sam's five-year-long chorus –
Is this trip necessary? – was *Oh yes,* my own voice most of all.
Off in the black Tudor sedan, a family united, we went
to recall another victory at Gettysburg, ground of a house divided.

We found the right graveyard at noon, a stone flat enough for our lunch
of turkey sandwiches with real butter, no longer rationed, hard boileds,
and post-war fudge. It was perfect – nothing but a boy with his belovèds.
And that evening, the first motel we'd seen – a separate cabin just for us.

Then it was *The Wizard of Oz* at the Majestic in new-fangled Technicolor.
The Wicked Witch melted, and glittering Glinda, the Good One,
showed me all it took to return to a happy home was a clicking

of heels three times, not the Gestapo jack-boot kind
I'd seen in newsreels and hoped never to see again
but those of our post-war Buster Browns and Oxfords.

4.25.21

The Brooding

for Kathy

Not Noah's branch-bearing dove,
certainly not a Holy Ghost come from Above,
this is just a Common Ground Dove, dun-colored.

Still, she pays attention to her work of incubating
three small white eggs on a patchwork of twigs
in a terracotta pot on my friend's porch,

hemmed in by garden tools planted in spent dirt.
Much has come from humble cabins and grain cribs.
May there be a opening here too, a rich beginning.

God knows we've had enough undoing, another friend
gone just the other day. The dove is named for her.
We must have birth.

5.29.21

Whose Porch This Is

for Kathy

She is leaning out her study window,
her wild cockade of hair streaked purple,
talking to two doves
on a porch railing a few feet from her,
not budging – as if they own the place.

The slightly rose-breasted male has joined
his dusky mate, the two of them revisiting
the digs where only recently they raised
their young, who are full-fledged now,
leaving room in the earthenware pot
where they nested . . .

except it's gone. The purple-streaked lady
has had it with the impropriety of birds
has removed the putrid pot, cleared its debris
and vacuumed up scads of scat on the porch
(a wasp nest to boot), reclaiming her place.
She is trying to explain her need to the doves.

They are not moved by her apology. He coos
that lovely serenade doves sing to say
they're here for good, plan four broods a year.
His throat pulses with the passion of his song.
For whom is it meant – his love or the lady –
while he eyes the porch for possibilities?

Will the nonagenarian with bird-bright hair
take them in? We'll see.

6.15.21

Firefly

And now the Sun, who fathered our primroses
all day, subsides, egging on the waxing moon.
Abed, basking in her light, nothing could be better,
we think, until suddenly the whole room lights up
so gold it seems the sun has moved in.

Like the strobing colors at a senior prom, the light
pulses on and off – a firefly
full of desire has found its way to our inner sanctum.
We celebrate in light of it.

6.20.21

Paradise Lost at the Retirement Center

for BJ

Like the Archangel Michael expelling Lucifer,
the Guardian of the Koi Pond Courtyard
storms out with a wild wing-sweeping
of her long arms and a stentorian "Get out,
get out, get out!" when she sees the disaster:

a bright-orange-vested grounds crew foreman
and his henchmen, disregarding the red stakes
protecting precious plantings from intrusion,
are tearing up armfuls
of milkweed carefully planted for Monarchs.

The dayglo intruders scatter
like the rebellious angel and his collaborators,
who fell to Earth in a dazzle of destructive fire
to do their earthly damage.

And now, just as the Archangel led a cleanup
of the quarters full of the stench and dirt
left behind by the rebels,
the Guardian goes straight to work
sweeping debris and planting Black-eyed Susans.

6.26.21

An Anniversary Remembered

Here where you and I hold hands beside this lush bog,
wood frogs gabble like small ducks
and fireflies blink –

bright souls of the dead, they say, maybe the Tunxis
who settled here, in league
with the land.

You're right — *blink* is not the word for it. Yes, *signal* –
a sort of prehistoric code: shorts and longs,
some brighter, some dimmer,

some low on the sward or in the sumac or among
the small Black Willow leaves
signaling *here, here.*

It's all one, how I trace the lines of your palm and how these
fire-beetles dot and dash their routes
above a bevy

of glow worms hidden in marsh grass and horsetail,
on stems of yellow-flag and loosestrife,
under jewel-weed – ladies

waiting for a sign, quick or languorous, bright or subtle,
long or blunt enough to be the one.
In light of such magic,

I tell you about the Night of Hotaru in Kyoto when
children fill their cheeks with fireflies to

shine like paper lanterns.

I love the way you allow wonder
to work in you
and love how we agree

the heavens floodlit with sheets of lightning
might be illuminated by some
enormous firefly.

7/16/21

The Art of Walking

At 1, Orlo navigates happily
stretching out his arms, waggling them
to maintain such new-found mobility.

At 85, like Karl Wallenda on high wire
strung many stories over a gawking
avenue, I too work my beamish arms

as a balancing pole dipping in salute
to the laws of physics, thanking them
for their suspension.

7.31.21

Loss

There was a time when loss was
just that, loss – easily remedied.
But these days Loss is capitalized.

Just now it's your spectacles –
brand new bifocals allowing you
to stay in touch – that are lost
"forever" you say through sobs.
How much keeps vanishing!

When we find the glasses teetering
on the top edge of a window sash
next to the Peace Lily you keep
from wilting away, you sob again
with delight and resolve:

you and I will be vigilant
and whatever losses accumulate
we will cling to our cliff,
keep our fingernails in fighting trim

8.8.21

Logging In

I pass time watching that little white circle spinning
on my monitor – celebrate my hiatus
in a sort of Tibetan trance.
Praised be the Dalai Lama's *say* that any circling thing
can be a prayer wheel – my PC's hard drive, for example,
and that little dotted circle spinning and spinning
its *om mani padme hum* of Compassion
out into the timeless Space where mantras travel –

Space in which the self dissolves
to a scattering of subatomic particles, rejoining its source
where songs might be born like star systems.
Thus I pass Time, happily going beyond it. Praised be
such intermissions, "white circle moments" between
bouts of business.

8.27.21

Replacement

for Marye Gail

As I write, my dear neighbor, you
have gone under, old bone removed
for a titanium knee. I pray for you

and for the wasp battering
the shut window by which I sit.
Into a plastic cup, oh wasp, you go,

and now into the cup of the world –
an omen for you, dear friend,
more limber than ever, racing Time.

9.3.21

Thelma

After the family has had its say
in memory of beloved Elizabeth,
Thelma, in a plain white shift
from her home in Jamaica,
blesses her employer:
"Mrs. Schley, she live forever!"

With which a squadron of Canada Geese
flies directly at the oak beneath which
her lady's ashes lie. The geese divide
into two squadrons at the ancient tree
then reunite beyond it. Thelma looks up
and nods to the Sky.

9.5.21

Roots

for Joan

How serpentine the writhe of
orchid roots, pale snarl of them.
But see the glory above,

as I did for weeks
when my dear, departed, left me
a favored orchid's mauve blooms:

weeks of lofty elegance
reminding me of hers
before the shriveled petal-fall.

Why I kept the potful of roots
God knows. Then one root rose
as if to take in the sun.

I watched, amazed, as it budded
and flowered, mauve
wing after wing of her unfurling.

9.15.21

Grades

3rd Grade already.
Such goings-on – sentences
and frogs dissected ... and
my affair with Babs Bowman,

who'd pierced my heart.
I yearned for a valentine made
in Crafts and placed in a heart-
shaped box on Miss P's desk.
I slipped in three for Babs.

Oh paradise lost the next year
when report cards ranked us
with grades I fought for
vs. *her*, smartest girl in 4th.

10.18.21

Inflation

for Kathy and George

She is deflated today,
92 after being happily 91 for so long.
And one rear tire of her scooter –
the Red Rover she races down halls
of this senior community – is flat.

She asks around. And George appears,
who renovates old cars (viz. the red Jag
splendid in the East Wing garage),
spirits off the wheel and *mirabile dictu*
returns with a red-ribboned one.

He takes a shot of her holding it.
Never has she looked so smart,
the purple streak in her hair on fire
like the stripe on a racing Ferrari.

10.23.21

The Clock and I

It too is a grandfather.
I visit each day to see if all's well
since it too has issues,
is compulsive, runs fast, abruptly
stops, needs me to hold its hand
and gently nudge it until we share
the time of day.

I wind the works
then tick the pendulum.
For the time being, not a second
separates us. It will not last
but I will keep at it.
Such labor love is, but O the worth!

10.28.21

The Lady and the Moose

for Margy

At our campsite on the Allagash
my friend Margy looked up
from her open-door outhouse seat

and saw a shaggy-bearded moose
pausing in his rounds to stare at her.
She closed her legs quickly and tried

to scream, unsuccessfully.
Back at the lean-to, she was speechless
until we got it out of her:

a moose
for God's sake!
We laughed her out of her shock

and loaded the canoes,
went on our whitewater way.
Next morning she told us her dream –

she and the moose each shone in
the wide eyes of the other,
a sharing.

11.4.21

The Lifting

In the grey time before dawn, my sins
pass before me, enormous, a stench, must do
their stint of heavy lifting – like so many
parading elephants tail to trunk, trunk to tail,
on their way to a huge canvas flat-out on
a dark fairground. The beasts strain, pull
ropes attached to three center poles,
and the canvas stirs, billows up . . .

The trapezes are lifted high, cubes are readied
for the performing seals, and soon the show
gives the lie to the dirt of the place.
Twenty clowns pile out of a tiny car, delighting,
and now a muscled man in shining tights catches
his beautiful partner midair. Around and around
they go, the bareback riders blowing kisses . . .

I rise for the day, getting on without a net.
I step out on a long line. I pray I will not fall again.

11.16.21

The Birthing

Of course there's room in the inn, she knows,
listening to her sharp-tongued mother's *No!*
Not for those out-of-town beggars.
Look, the girl's water has already broken –
we'd have a mess. Straw's good enough for them.

She waits until her parents' door has shut,
quickly boils a pot of water, finds shears,
and heads into a blinding dust storm . . .

In the barn the girl's already in labor, straining,
the man helpless. She's seen birth, sheep mainly,
knows to take the crowning head in both hands,
into which he slips, brown and, as she proclaims,

"perfect." She cuts the cord, washes the strangely
serene child, wraps him in a new saddle blanket.
The girl is too young, she thinks, but radiant.

11.28.21 (first day of Advent)

A Meditation on Time

"Hurry up, please, it's time," says the barman
closing up shop in Eliot's *Waste Land*. "Please,
just one more whiskey," a regular sings out.

Here, far from a London pub, we understand
the domination of Time. The halls of the home
are crowded with grandfather clocks.

Some of us want their works stopped, unnerved
by all that ticking and chiming—like whoever
stole the key to the clock by the eatery,

maybe thinking his condition wouldn't progress
in a timeless world where not only the hours
but even the cycles of sun and moon are halted.

I want the opposite: for Time to continue ticking,
its hands moving like mine
which do the daily things that keep me going,

like my job of winding one of the grandfathers.
Unhappily, my hands move unsteadily: I drop
the wind-up key into the deep recesses of the old

time-keeper and am rescued only by the loan
of a long "picker-upper" that justifies its name.
My ticker's content. I can breathe again.

11.28.21

Blood Moon Over the Cathedral

The round wafer of the Blood Moon
silhouettes the steeple of the cathedral.
Its cross is invisible, turned sideways
as if God is elsewhere.

By day, the tall steeple is undergoing
restoration. Sliced open, it reveals
a cell tower within, transmitting
words, words, words, but not the Word.

Now, looked at from another angle,
the cross flashes, has its say, its arms
more substantial than the stubby limbs
of the buzzing cell tower below.

12.2.21

A Prayer for Advent

The over-sized Christmas ornaments gaudily
hanging by the almost frozen pond
cannot make up for water lilies gone,
a defunct enamel turtle undone by UV
and the elegant white cat not in her window,
deceased yesterday after weeks of holding on.

A gang of boring brown sparrows gorging
and fat pigeons turning porches to outhouses
are a disappointment.

May I be jolted from bleak December doldrums
by the advent of goldfinch in winter costumes
apter than glittery ornaments. O finches,
come from the spent meadow where you lament.

Come Christmasly, demi-gilt or olive,
Come with beaks keen to take in thistle-seed,
chirping amicably, feasting at this manger
like your kin at another two thousand years ago.

12.8.21

Solstice Celebration in a Time of Pandemic

It is Winter Solstice, time to beat back the dark
with noise-making. I blow a bird whistle
making the raucous kree of a red-tailed;
another beats a copper pot with a soup spoon;
a third rings a ship bell.

On our 5th floor corridor at the retirement center
this night of nights, we're fine feathered
in our multicolored duds and fancy doodads,
one in bare feet and pj's, one up from a lower level,
looking for kindred souls.

Deep down is a dark we would undo
with our December Mardi-gras'ing. Beyond revelry,
Death stalks our corridors, the Virus bringing in
reinforcements daily. And even without the coup
de grâce of plague, endings are endemic here. Truth is

we're making our ruckus to rout extinction,
putting a hex on whatever afflicts our dear ones,
banging away at disaster.

12.22.21

Another Birth

By chance I listened to the news
Christmas morning. It was all about
the take-over of a new Virus strain

until, miracle of miracles, it turned
to the launching of a space telescope
so powerful it will look into the origin

of Everything. Traveling in its Space
bubble, a womb of sorts, it is slowly
unwrapping itself, extending its limbs.

Delivered to its ultimate station
a million miles from Earth, it will see
so deeply into Space and Time

we will perhaps realize how miraculous
and infinitely minute our planet is –
how we had best bow down in prayer.

12.26.21

Praise Song for Skunk Cabbage

The skunk cabbage and I are in cahoots –
we know true spring starts early in January
as the sun edges north. *Winter begone*
say the cabbage and I as it augers greenly up
through the dead leaves of yesteryear,
burning a circle of melt through ice and snow.

The green heavenward twist of the spicy fetid
Symplocarpus foetidus is a consolation
as it flushes purple, luring early flyers in love with
the sweet stink of decay, creating a warm boudoir

for its lascivious guests. I know – it is as inhuman
as the spiky burr of the Virus decimating humanity.
Happily, its persistence is an argument for God
or at least that Explosion of stars and galaxies
of which we are a short-lived part.

1.8.22

Joy

In the bleak midwinter desperation
of an ambulance, crying out in pain
at every jounce, she cries out in joy,
staring wide-eyed out a window
at the day's blue emptiness of sky –

"Oh look, how white the moon!"
The old woman holds up a figment
between her thumb and forefinger
and blows on it like sending the fluff
of a dandelion sailing into heaven.

1.11.22

Connection

It fizzled yesterday, my connection to the web –
no music, no phone, no send/receive, no Roku . . .
I was left to my own devices, not my provider's
smart ones, but another's.

I'm reconnected today – except for the nagging
of some prehistoric part of me that says, "Let's go
outside and play like Wizard leaping through his
electronic fence, cavorting with the dog next door."

1.13.22

The Waiting

for Sarah

First sight at dawn, she's tightly swaddled
in blankets pulled around her,
seems bound for the Egyptian Underworld...

except the wraps are closer to a silk moth's
cocoon. The slightest stir's within.
I rise and wait, relying on coffee and biscuit,

collecting the least crumbs
with a fingertip, tasting them, savoring
all that's left – most of all her, remembering

how she reached deep in the womb of a ewe,
turned the lamb, pulled him out by the forelegs;
how she dug buried spuds, held them up to view.

I am willing her to break free of her wrappings,
come back to me to taste the elixir I offer
and drink day in once more, no underworld for her.

1.21.22

ABOUT THE AUTHOR

Rennie McQuilkin was Poet Laureate of Connecticut from 2015 through 2018. His work has appeared in *The Atlantic, Poetry, The Southern Review, The Yale Review, The Hudson Review, The American Scholar, Crazyhorse,* and elsewhere. This is his nineteenth poetry collection. He has received a number of awards for his work, including fellowships from the National Endowment for the Arts and the Connecticut Commission on the Arts, as well as a Lifetime Achievement Award from the Connecticut Center for the Book. In 2010 his volume of new and selected poems, *The Weathering,* was awarded the Center's annual poetry prize under the aegis of the Library of Congress; and in 2018, *North of Eden* received the Next Generation Indie Book Award in Poetry. For nine years he directed the Sunken Garden Poetry Festival, which he co-founded at Hill-Stead Museum in Farmington, Connecticut. With his wife, the artist Sarah McQuilkin, he lives at Seabury in Bloomfield, CT.

This book is set in Garamond Premier Pro, which had its genesis in 1988 when type-designer Robert Slimbach visited the Plantin-Moretus Museum in Antwerp, Belgium, to study its collection of Claude Garamond's metal punches and typefaces. During the fifteen hundreds, Garamond – a Parisian punch-cutter – produced a refined array of book types that combined an unprecedented degree of balance and elegance, for centuries standing as the pinnacle of beauty and practicality in type-founding. Slimbach has created a new interpretation based on Garamond's designs and on compatible italics cut by Robert Granjon, Garamond's contemporary.

Copies of this book can be ordered
directly from Rennie McQuilkin
400 Seabury Dr., Apt. 5196
Bloomfield, CT 06002.
Send $18 per book
plus $4 shipping
by check payable
to Antrim House.

•

For more information on the work of Rennie McQuilkin
visit www.antrimhousebooks.com/authors.html.
The author can be contacted at
RMcQuil36@gmail.com
860-519-1804.

CPSIA information can be obtained
at www.ICGtesting.com
Printed in the USA
JSHW021245020322
23424JS00003B/4